POEMS AND PRAYERS

for

W̶INTER

by
Mary
Fleeson

G000273513

The days are shorter now,
The sun barely warms.
I am not yet ready
And the night is here.

Grey leaden skies,
Heavy with gloom,
Threaten my equilibrium
And feed a maudlin mood.

I reach for comfort,
Fluffy blanket warmth,
Cosy fake-fur slippers
And brimming mug of tea.

In the quiet I find peace,
Wrapped in promises
Of endings and beginnings
Times and seasons.

IT WAS YOU WHO SET ALL THE BOUNDARIES OF THE EARTH; YOU MADE BOTH SUMMER AND WINTER. PSALM 74:17

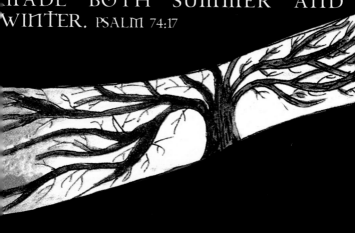

And in knowing that the Seasons are God-given,

Winter may become a gift to some,

 - help me to offer help where the cold is feared.

And in knowing that the stars will shine for longer,

Winter may becomes a wonder to some,

 - help me to offer help where the night is too long.

And in knowing that the land is recovering,

Winter may become a comfort to some,

 - help me to offer help where turmoil overwhelms.

FOR AS THE RAIN AND THE SNOW COME
DOWN FROM HEAVEN, AND DO NOT RETURN
THERE WITHOUT WATERING THE EARTH
AND MAKING IT BEAR AND SPROUT, AND
FURNISHING SEED TO THE SOWER AND
BREAD TO THE EATER; SO WILL MY WORD BE
WHICH GOES FORTH FROM MY MOUTH; IT
WILL NOT RETURN TO ME EMPTY, WITHOUT
ACCOMPLISHING WHAT I DESIRE.

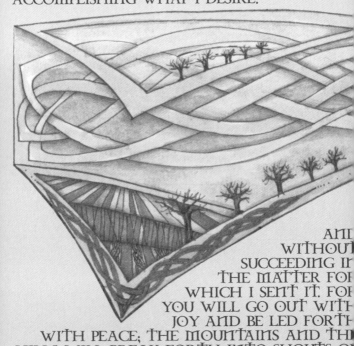

AND
WITHOUT
SUCCEEDING IN
THE MATTER FOR
WHICH I SENT IT. FOR
YOU WILL GO OUT WITH
JOY AND BE LED FORTH
WITH PEACE; THE MOUNTAINS AND THE
HILLS WILL BREAK FORTH INTO SHOUTS OF
JOY BEFORE YOU, AND ALL THE TREES OF
THE FIELD WILL CLAP THEIR HANDS
ISAIAH 55:10-1

The seasons, Spring to Winter.
Life, birth to death.
Our awareness of the cycle of things,
Tells us that nothing is really wasted,
No time is unnecessary,
No life is expendable,
No word unheeded,
No love unneeded.

But time can be misplaced
In a multitude of frustrating ways,
And life can be diminished,
We know that to be true.
Words can be silenced and love rejected.
So where is Hope in this Wintry despair?
It shelters in the laugh of an innocent child,
Finds refuge in the promises fulfilled
And love unconditional, in the birdsong
And the prayers of those who cherish,
And the actions of those who dare
To do His will.

In the cold of this misty-breath night,
I will look to the moon and pause,
and know that You created it
from the same dust that made me.

In the darkness of this indigo-velvet night,
I will look to the moon and wonder,
and worship You in humility
for You gave us Light in our darkness.

In the stillness of this ice-cold night,
I will look to the moon and pray,
and give thanks to You
for Your love and many mercies.

MAY THE GOD OF HOPE FILL YOU WITH
ALL JOY AND PEACE AS YOU TRUST IN HIM,
SO THAT YOU MAY OVERFLOW WITH HOPE
BY THE POWER OF THE HOLY SPIRIT.
ROMANS 15:13

Cool Winter sun,
Usurper of the golden throne,
Your false promises of warmth
Are like the affections of the deceiver
Hollow and trivial!

But look at the trees,
In this Season they are vulnerable,
But mighty in their naked beauty,
They give shelter unconditionally
Even as they are exposed.

May I be more like the trees...

Makes me shiver, just remembering,
The bitter winds, the swirling skies
And blizzard snows.
Such beauty though, in the contrasting light,
The virgin blanket, the crisp edges
And frozen shore.

Makes me shiver, just imagining,
The awestruck shepherds, the dazzling angels
And ethereal alleluias.
Such fear though, of that celestial light,
The virgin birth, the Holy babe
And a world transformed.

HE SAYS, "BE STILL, AND KNOW THAT I AM GOD" PSALM 46:10

Do the trees wait patiently for the Spring,
Or does the sap keep still reluctantly
Like a wriggling toddler longing to explore?
Is the Winter a prison of sorts,
Holding nature to ransom
Until the sun pays in heat?

When I wait for an understanding of God,
Am I reluctant to be still and listen,
Unable to accept the challenge of quiet?
Do I limit the time I can spare?
Do I hold Him to ransom?
Until my wayward inner child grows up?

iamond display,
eavens heralding
hrist child,
tatus: Saviour,
orn to transform all.

rystal clear,
rosty firmament,
tarlit skies,
ontemplate: continuing,
n the same old way.

orn tonight,
etween belief
nd apprehension.
hose: Christ,
nd the universe shifted.

HELP
ME
TO
KNOW
THAT
WITH
YOUR
HELP,
SOMEHOW,
IN
SOME
SMALL
WAY,
I
CAN
MAKE
A
DIFFERENCE.
AMEN

Freezing rain trickles down my neck,
Defying my attempt at keeping dry.
I am transported,
By that cold reminder,
To Winters of the past,
Of rushing from indoor place to indoor place,
Slushy half-melted snow splashing where I tread,
Orange street lights and shop windows reflecting,
The sharp smell of snow-laden air competing,
With diesel fumes as a bus goes by.

A shiver of awareness ripples down my back,
An unbidden call to my spirit perhaps.
I am shown,
Through divine eyes,
The Winter of my heart,
How I have avoided, in my rushing around,
People I could have helped or cared about,
I see now the tears in His eyes brimming,
In my little world this and that competing,
Has pushed Him further away.

Pause, and take shelter,
From the Winter rain,
See it make tracks
Down the window pane.
Play that game...
Which droplet will get there first?
Thank God that life is not a race.

Pause, and rest for now,
From the Winter wind,
Hear it howl and whistle
Through the trees.
Remember the disciples...
And the Holy Spirit like the wind.
Thank God that we can still receive.

Tales of kindness follow the humble Robin.
Did he fan the fire in the birthing room
where Jesus lay?
Was his breast stained red by the blood
from the thorny crown?
We cannot go back in time to help the Holy Family,
Or ease Christ's suffering on the cross,
But in serving others,
We serve Him.

TRULY I TELL
YOU,
WHATEVER
YOU DID
FOR ONE OF
THE LEAST
OF THESE
BROTHERS
AND SISTERS
OF MINE,
YOU DID
FOR ME.
MATTHEW 25:40